This page has been left blank intentionally.

Dream Dreams

A journey through life's movements
outlined in poetry

Sandra Pollock

SanRoo Publishing
ISBN No: 978-0-9957078-0-1

www.SanRoopublishing.co.uk
www.sandrapollock.com

First published in paperback edition
By SanRoo publishing 2017

The right of Sandra Pollock

to be identified as the author of this work has been asserted under the
Copyright, Designs and Patents Act 1988.

All rights reserved.

No part of this publication may be reproduced, stored in a retrieval system
or transmitted in any form, by any means, digital, electronic, photocopy,
recorded or otherwise, without the prior written consent of the publisher,
nor be otherwise circulated in any form by binding or cover other than that
in which it is published without a similar condition including this condition
being imposed on the subsequent purchaser.

Designed by Sandra Pollock

Typeset by Sandra Pollock for SanRoo Publishing

Cover Image: Sandra Pollock

Cover design Copyright ©Sandra Pollock 2016

This edition in paperback format copyright ©2016 SanRoo Publishing,
26 Bramble Way, Leicester, LE3 2GY, Leicestershire, UK

ISBN 978-0-9957078-0-1

Contents Index

Acknowledgements	5
Welcome To My Journey Into Poetic Creativity	6
A Daughter's Tale	7
Flowers in the Field of Humanity	9
Not Been There Lately	10
To My Dear Sister	11
To Write Without Regret	13
What Do I Write About?	14
Woman, Divine	15
Write the Words	16
You are unique	18
New Cards Fell	19
Dream Dreams	20
I'm Looking At Myself Today.	21
I've Written To You	22
I Live For You	23
Sometimes You Have To	25
So You Thought	26
The Art of Being Me	28
The Sea Hill	29
Things Don't Always	31
Just Because	33
Life's Path	35
Life, Duz Change	37
Dis Skin I Living In	39
Satadee Cleaning	40
To Go Forward	42
Touch	44
What If	45
With You I am Alive	47
A Message To Somebody…	48
About the Author	50
Social Media Links	51
SanRoo Publishing	52

Acknowledgements

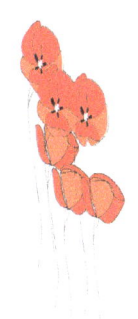

To my beautiful, intelligent and creative daughter Jerusha, thank you for taking my dreams and returning them to me filled with even more life, vitality and inspiration, that has renewed them within me again. You are my delight.

To Mike Pollock, ours has been a journey of change. Thank you for joining me for the ride and for your patience, love and belief. Thanks for being there when I was struggling with the detail of this publication, wanting to learn to do everything myself. Ever and Always.

To the goddess that is Carol Leeming, your light so shines that all it touches, even for the briefest of moments are forever changed for the better. Thank you for your encouragement, support and example of one who follows her dreams fiercely, tenaciously, and achieves them all without fear.

To Sonia Thompson, thank you for being there when many others fell by the wayside. I could not ask for more. Your friendship and commitment means everything. To Nirmala Bhojani, you are truly an inspirational woman. To Janet Walton who came to my rescue as I learnt how to set this book.

All of you - Thank you from my heart! Our sisterhood has paved the way for so much more than we imagined at the start. Words can never be enough, but I promise to keep writing them in appreciation.

To the many other women, friends and supporters that have made my journey of personal discovery possible. This is also for you, so that you may know that nothing is impossible and it is worth it all to dream your dreams and to pursue them until you hold them firmly with love, joy and accomplishment in your own hands.
With love always, dream dreams, change the world.

Welcome To My Journey Into Poetic Creativity

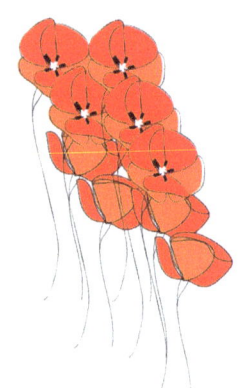

I have long written all sorts of genre, for work, for pleasure, for fun or just for the sake of. Much of my writing has been to expel the thought, pain, pleasure, passion, and many other of the emotional experiences life brings to share with us.

These poems are really stories that have come to me and been compiled over the years. During periods of huge change, personal exploration and awakening to myself and who I'm to be.

The putting of them together into this book is another act on my part of allowing myself to be free, to dream my dreams, to be me.

Some, I am sure will make sense or even find a connection within you. Others may just appear to be the passing of pictures, the painting of life, colours and words that fit together in only a fraction of the second it takes to create a thought.

Whatever comes to you as you read through what is only my creative thoughts, I hope you will allow them to form in even greater colours, pictures and visions within you, and that this takes you further along your unique life journey.

Thank you for joining me in my travels into my poetic creativity.

May you find inspiration as I have. Sending you love & light.

Sandra

A Daughter's Tale

It is hard for us to talk these days; it's hard for us to share.
Although we remain so far apart, the hardest thing to face,
Is how little you know of me right now, how much I have achieved,
How little you are aware of the strength, within I breathe.

The inspiration: the effect you've weaved,
The results of your hard work,
That's made my life a reflection of what you have achieved.
How little you are aware of that inspiration,
The effect your life has made on me,
All of which I'm proud to say,
I will not regret or leave.

I wanted just to say although we never talk,
That you have been my inspiration,
Your strength and power of thought.
To see your ambition and resilience,
Persistence over the years,
The many things you've tried and did,
The strength that did appear.

This will not change the here and now
For nothing I regret
But I can still find inspiration
And let you know before too late
To say although we never talk, the things I can't forget
To be an inspiration now myself
Your legacy to invest.

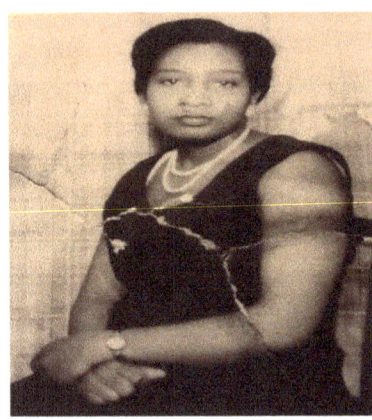

My mother, Eulalie Herring (nee Watson) around the age of 19 when she first arrived in the UK from Barbados.

Written to my mother at a time when we struggled to communicate, speak, or share: to be together in unity.
Long before the time that is now, when communication in the form we take for granted ceased to be.
Never-the-less, my mother has and will always be an amazing woman, an inspiration.
My prayer for my experience with my daughter, is that we always have a better level of communication throughout our lives.

Flowers in the Field of Humanity

You're beautiful, and when I look at you all,
I see flowers in the field of humanity.

Different hues, different shapes and sizes, different jewels,
All beautifully individual, unique and fantastic to see.

Each with different gifts to give,
Attractions to view, smells to intoxicate, the senses so sweet,
Flowers in the field of humanity.

Each man, woman and child I see,
Is a reflection of me?

A reminder of how one but different,
The Creator has made us to be,
Flowers in the field of humanity.

A reflection of the Infinity's love
For creativity, expansion,
The gift to be free,
Flowers in the field of humanity.

To up root one is to change the landscape,
Is to spoil the beauty that makes this all unique,
A vision, a reflection of one far greater than we,
Who has made all of creation a treasure to seek,
Flowers in the field of humanity.

Not Been There Lately

It's been a while, not been in touch
Life's full of changes: the occasionally too much.
Have you been busy, kept writing in time,
Created some amazing stuff for us to join in and chime?
People die, life keeps changing,
Stuff to deal, not always just meditating.
But the changes in life gives you things about which to write
Things to learn from, things you ignite.

It's never clear when people have not been there,
What might be happening,
What they can't share,
And there are things and reasons too,
Why you may never know.
It's not the place you get to go to,
You may even think that they don't care,
When they are not around,
Your issues to share.

But even when not present,
Not sharing the physical and its essence,
They may well be there,
In thought and spirit,
Their things you think are just not in it.
But more may be or even closer,
Never feel forsaken when,
We don't move closer,
We've not been there lately,
Well, not sort of.

To My Dear Sister

To my dear sister,
Just wanted to drop you a note,
To share my readiness to give you my 100% vote.
To encourage you to take a chance,
To trust another and you play out this dance.

None of us remains the same,
None of us can ever remain the same.
We either grow up or we grow down,
We either grow more entrenched or we expand,
We either decide to smile or to frown.

Life is waiting for you to play your hand.
Life is a place of movement,
Of continual choice, of taking chances,
Of sharing your voice, of accepting the dances.

Where we either burn with desire, with passion and hope,
Or we shy away from growing into the glory with which we can cope,
But each step is a decision,
You make a choice to become,
Vulnerable with growth or hold back and choke,
On what is really your own greatness,

That can only shine when you take those chances,
To be open, defenceless, exposed.
It's only here that your power is grown.
Your power to learn, to become stronger,
To trust, to love, to grow, to hack it.

In you is the glorious inspirational package,
That is needed by others their journey to manage.
So, choose well my sister and know for sure,
That I have your back, as I know for sure that you have mine.

Come on, and let's get with it, my dear sister, friend and inspiration,
We are entwined.

My beautiful sister Marna Scott and I in Barbados.

To Write Without Regret

To write without regret,
To live without upset,
To wish no boundaries existed
And yet,
But knowing the safety of such a net.

To realise the truth of oneness,
Therefore, there is nothing hidden.
Nothing out of reach, nothing forbidden, none.

Knowing the love one feels,
Whatever the focus of one's objectives revealed,
Is pure within its need,
It is only the actions that can corrupt such purity.

Boundaries exist to protect me,
Limits abound to control thee,
Life continues to create in order for me to truly see,
Who indeed I am within me.

What Do I Write About?

What do I write about? I've been asked.
Where do I start? What is my path?
Write about what you know,
Write about where you are,
Write what you've suffered in life,
What's your start? Where do you go?

Respect your journey, Respect your sight,
Your opinion, your choices,
Respect your right.
The best messages are those from your heart,
Those that are real to you,
They are those which leave a mark.

What do you write about?
Only you can say, only you have your vision,
And know how you play.

What do you write about?
Well that is the prize,
Only you can see the world through your own eyes.
So, don't be afraid, your view is valid,
Speak up sister, brother,
Join the allied, write from here.

Woman, Divine

Channel of the Divine,
Priestess, Goddess, Woman,
Made to create, the word given.

Mother, Creator, Carer, Guide.
Power to all who walk by her side.
Governess of all with whom she resides.
Powerful, Knowing, Seer, Hope,
Healer,
Provider with the Infinite scope.

Wisdom, success, abundance renewed.
The One, the Beautiful, the True.

A woman iridescence of the creator's road.
Can only true love, light and wisdom bestow,
To separate at heart and mind.
To speak and think, wise, power, unfold and reap.
Mean responsibility to bear,
The words of lesser, dangers created she bears.

Come away now to be all that the Creator has placed in thee
Woman, Channel of the Divine
Only love, light and beauty on all to shine.

Write the Words

Write the words,
Find the voice,
List the things you would include.
Lift the trumpet,
Sound the noise
For all you would introduce.

State the value,
Make the point,
So, that you might stand out.
Shine the light,
Show the candle
Bring every woman in from without.

Doors open up,
Spread windows wide.
Bring in the change for all.
Women standing out,
Who bring no doubt
Their succession feeds one and all.

Find the right,
Ignite the fight,
Bring truth and light to dim.
Show the way,
Exalt the day,
So, all in truth stand tall.

Make a choice,
Use strength and noise,
To bring equality in.

For she is who from whom
We all are born,
Yourself you do deny,
If she you fight
The life her power gave,
The love she did supply.

Write the words, sound the voice
And justice will it sing out.
Shine the light, show the candle
So, all can stand up and equality may
Sit within, without.

You are unique

You are unique.
I know you've heard it said before,
But clearly you need to hear it some more,
You are unique.

You are unique, You're the only one,
Like you on this on this planet,
The only one.
There will never be another just like you,
No, it just cannot be done.

So, believe in yourself, Believe in your worth,
Allow the gifts you have to be unearthed,
To spread and fly like Dandelion seeds,
Skipping through the air and over open fields.

To find a true resting place in other hearts and minds,
Allow your unique, your powerful light to shine,
Your awesomeness to unwind,
You are unique.

You are unique, believe it's true,
Believe for me, believe for you, Believe for others
In all you do, believe in you.
Yes, you're awesome, that cannot be changed.
So, just work with it, you can make the grade.
Allow your uniqueness to remain.
And join with me in this glad refrain.
I am unique, this is my name.

New Cards Fell

I woke up this morning, in a new land.
Brought here by fate, the stroke of life's hand,
I thought I was here for one reason,
But others appeared and shook up,
What I had balanced in my hands.

And as the new cards fell,
In these I, could not tell what I was to do,
Everything was now new,
So, unexpected, so wonderful and true,
So much what I wanted to feel and to do.

All though forbidden,
Supposing to be out of reach,
All of what my heart, my being beckoned,
Longed for, needed.

Were I to accept this strange new deal,
What would the future hold?
What would this reveal?

To forget the old and cleave to the new,
Is so very thrilling, so exciting to do.
But life is not so easy, not so easy to do,
Too many others depending on you.

Some sacrifice, some sadness, somewhere,
Either your heart or theirs.
A decision, almost impossible to dare.

Dream Dreams

Dream dreams that call you,
That draw you, that pull you,
Out of your darkness and into your shining light,
That gives you the tools to create,
A world that will bring you,
A Life, an existence that's right for you,
To be your truest self: the you, that shines so bright.

Dream dreams that call you,
Dream the biggest, the boldest dreams,
Those that challenge your fears,
Those that make you dry your tears,
Those that make you sing,
That resurrect the highest spark of life itself in you.

Dream dreams that call you,
That draw you, that pull you into,
Who you've planned here in your imagination to be,
To form upon this earth and see.

Dream dreams that guide you,
That make you move even when you'd like only to snooze.
Dream dreams that create a path,
That you have no choice but to follow through,
That craft a unique track for the likes of me and you,
To want to see and do,
Go on now, dream your dreams,
The dreams that you alone can dream.

I'm Looking At Myself Today.

I'm looking at myself today and wondering where I've been,

Where I'm going to get to, not without, but within.

Finding myself is such a treasure,

One that's ever new,

As I grow on, learning more about me,

I find out so much more that's true.

I'm looking at myself today,

And amazed at what I see,

Sometimes I can't believe that this awesome person is me.

Full of promise, full of dreams, full of so many things.

If only I could learn to listen to my spirit more, the eternal lover within.

I'm looking at myself today,

And each day I'm more sure,

Of my mission, here upon this earth, the things I'm here to do, to explore.

To leave this place much better,

Than it was the moment I came,

To grace this earth with my physical colours and tunes and shades.

I'm looking at myself today and I'm glad I have more time,

To make a greater impact on the world that is mine,

To shine.

I've Written To You

I've written to you time and again,
Of my undying love with no end.
I've written of my longing desire,
My unchanging need to be in your arms,
To hear your breath upon my skin.

I've written and still the words come,
Flowing out and over and over about me,
Rolling out of me, my heart and my mind,
A flowing out of all that is divine.

This calling, these words are endless and true,
But only copies of the love that is within me for you.
This life, this moment to capture,
To hold for a second, to know again, after.

I've written to you, time and again,
And still there is no limit, no place to begin.
It is as if I've loved you forever,
Yet waited till now to share the favour.
It is as if as one we have always been,
Interrupted in time this love again to proceed,
A love story halted now to begin anew.

I've written to you time and again,
To this unending love of which I now sing,
To tell you again the story of our time, our end.
Together again in this life entwined,
Another time of our love to share, to shine,
Another moment of adventure to dare,
And so, I've written to you time and again.

I Live For You

I Feel alive, this is what you do,
The sound of your voice,
The music of you.

The warmth of your breath, reaching my flesh,
Awakening every hair on my skin – no protest within,
I draw ever closer to you, any chance,
Unable to resist this sexual dance.

Your scent in my nostrils, I drink in your breath;
It flows down into my being, taking me to bed,
Awakening every cell within me,
My entire being is spent.

Like nothing I have ever known,
All, every inch of me involved,
Writhing and reaching, yearning for you,
Now what do I do, I'm lost in the wanting of you.

I look at your picture and even this is fire,
And my heart, my breast, my innermost parts are desire,
Are awakened entirely, yearning for you,
All a-dew.

The manfulness of how you do,
All the things to me you do,
I live for you.

Only wanting to have you, reaching for you,
Every masculine bit of you.
My mind is a fog of mist,
Sex and love and wanting
Unable to think clearly to climb, not wanting to.

Before you knew, this was my state,
Unable to do without seeing you, unable to wait.

And now that I'm with you,
I still cannot get enough
Of the powerful way that you love,
The manfulness of how you do,
All the things you to me you do,
In deed, I live for you.

Sometimes You Have To

Sometimes you have to make a choice,
Sometimes you have to bow out,
Step away from the noise,
Move into the calm,
We all have a choice.

It's not that you don't care,
It's not like you're not there to hear the screams,
To see the cries and the pain,
To recoil from the call of the names.

It's just that for balance,
For tranquillities,
To be able to actually help,
Sometimes you have to breathe.

Take your own breath,
To avoid the drowning of the sea of suffering,
The never ending distractions from the truth,
The truth of who we are, really.
We all need to, at times remember,
The better part of who we are within,
And what we believe most about ourselves,
That, we will become.

So You Thought

So you thought you had achieved,
The ultimate of spiritual growth and divine unity.
But then something unexpected,
Is thrown into the mix,
Of what you called your good life, your made bed,
And now you know not who you are or what to do instead.

Could you have imagined,
Where you find yourself now,
Lost, uncertain, full of unbridled passion and how?
For life laughs at you,
At this place, you find yourself in.
Saying, now who are you to judge, to play your way thin?

Only life is in control,
And you just have to learn to roll,
With the throw of the dice,
With the glow of the light,
With a decision, a thought, a 'I just might',
With the appearance of the rainbow or the night.

You have no control,
Even though you'd like to pretend that you can choose,
Where you can go to, where to end; to win or lose,
Now that would truly be power,
But what would you learn then?
And how would you be there to help others sojourn?

Just roll with the punches.
Flow with the glow of love,
Wherever it takes you.
Just go with it now, why not?

And be not afraid of this new day,
It's all working out great, it will any way.
By the movement of the Life's hand.
By the joys of the sun's rays,
By the controller, by life itself.

Though you thought, differently.
Life is not what you thought,
And it cannot be undone.

The Art of Being Me

The art of being me,
The art of being you,
There is no real art in being me or being you.

It's art if there is one, is in being true,
Not being afraid to do what you want to do,
To be who you want to be,
That's the art of being me.

If an artist of my life I am to be,
Comes from the strength of being free,
I find the more I do whatever it is that pleases me,
When I set myself free, from the judgement of others to just be,
The less pressure I place on me, you see,
I then delight in being me.

The art of being me is in learning to be free,
Within my mind, within my heart.
It's the beginning, it's where we all start.

The art of being me is in truly learning,
That to be me is to be free.

The Sea Hill

Early every morning, before the sun appears,
The breezes arrive at the nape of the hill,
The waves wash ashore with the gentle crashing,
The splashing against the rocks,
The dashing.

In the crocks of Cove Bay,
Just enough space for a fisherman to moor,
For a bather to wash his body, play and adorn,
Away from the tourist loom and the heat of the day sun.

Sitting still on a rock, the grass or beneath,
The Sea Grape tree at her feet,
Just looking out and enjoying the breeze,
The sound of the wind,
The beautiful ocean scene

The beauty of the expanse of sky
And ocean, meeting together, creating,
Love's portion here by.

To connect with nature, with the heaven and the earth,
To touch the grass, the trees and the soil, is new birth.
To enjoy the stillness of what is to us,
A gift that locals hide and keep in their trust.

The Sea Hill, where by grandmother and hers
With countless others too,
Have travelled, have walked, have sat and enjoyed
On this earth,
And never failed their attentions and time to give.
Just a stroll away from the house,
Where we've lived, where we have loved.
Offers all a dose of quietness and harmony,
Of heavenly love and peace.
A chance to touch the souls position,
To remember the gift of heaven's rendition.

Things Don't Always

Things don't always turn out
As you would have hoped,
But things always turn out
Some way or another.

The thing is to adjust.
Now that is the hard part to stand.
How do you adjust?
How do you work that out?
When your heart, your mind and your body, short
Are all asking and wanting something different,
To be about.

There are all sort of names,
For this mental, physical and emotional imbalance,
But no name changes it.

The darkness may be the darkest,
You may have seen,
The darkness may be the darkest
You've ever felt,
The darkness may be the darkest
You've ever known.
You can't touch it, but you feel it,
You can't touch it, but it touches you.

It confuses you,
Where is the light?
You may see the occasional spark,
But the tunnel of change can be the darkest dark,
But you can't turn back,
You can't stop the process,
You can't halt the change.
You can only hope for rest.

Just let it happen, just let it come,
Whatever is arriving, nothing else can be done.

Confusion, grief, disappointment,
Frustration, loss of fulfilment,
Life's like a delusion.
Nothing is sure any more, nothing is safe,
No one can be trusted, life's playing her game.

But things will turn out, they always have to,
Don't allow this confusion,
To turn you out.
It's just a part of what we must live through,
And the realisation that even you,
Don't really know you or your life path.

Just Because

Just because you've never heard it,
Does not mean you can't do it now.
Just because you've never seen it,
Does not mean you can't show them how.

Just because it's not been done before,
Doesn't mean it will not succeed.
Just because it's not been said before,
Doesn't mean truth is not revealed.

Just because you're not an adult yet,
Does not withhold your strength.
Just because your colour is different,
Does not deny your depth.

Just because is no excuse, no reason not to try.
Just because you are alive your call is justified.
There is no other why.
Just because will always be enough until the day you die.

Just because you have the thought,
Gives you reason to clarify.
Just because you have an idea,
Is all the reason why you try.
Just because you're here and now means,
You've something special to give, to provide.
Just because, that makes you special.
We wait for the gifts your breathe.

Just because is all the reason
You're required to be unique.
For the good of all around, of you and me,
To use your voice and all you have to speak.

Just because the road is not clear,
Does not mean you're lost.
Just because you're doing something different,
Does not mean yours is not a cause.
Just because your light shines brighter,
Does not mean you should hold back,
Just because your way seems restricted,
Does not mean you're not on track.

Just because you it's getting harder,
Is no reason to refrain.
Just because you choose not see me,
Compels me to remain.
Just because you do not hear me
Does not mean I do not care.
Just because we're disconnected
From who we really are,
Does not mean I'm not doing for you
All I am required.

Just because, Just because, Just because…

Life's Path

Launched, grown, reaching into the sand,
The soil and the water.
Strength of the planned;
Strength of the making, golden and complete.

Reaching up, reaching out,
Standing firm, holding deep,
The cradle that forms and creates life;
This is the dawn, the place of light,
Given forth into the sandal of life.

How strong this beat of passion,
How strong this beat of compassion,
How strong the pain some refusal reposes.

Knowing, being part of all,
The river, the air, the water, the sand,
The soil, the plants – the life.

The bowl, the cradle,
The ball, the global, the universal womb,
Bringing into the physical all things,
From that which is unseen, the powerful hidden.
Raising up, growing out towards the stars.
How tall, how strong, how giving, how being –
How bright is life.

There is the Sun,
Without form, without limit –
Just being, just emitting.

From the feet, growing upwards,
From the foundations; ever glowing,
Ever changing, ever becoming, ever knowing,
Ever higher into the knees.

To the womb, to hold and to make something new;
To hold in the heart; to feed from breast,
To lick and kiss with tongue and lips.

To hold and to release, to chasten, to chase;
Only to return to the river, the water,
The air, the soil – to the birth, to the gift of Life.

Life, Duz Change

Hey, life duz change, it duz change a lot,
You really don't own anyting you got,
It just wat you need for dis part of dee journey,
Ta help wid ya living and ya learning.

We not meant to remain da same.
We meant to grow, and learn and change.
It's wen you feel you got it made,
Life trow you a curve ball, ta mek you change.

Growing truu all dee hoods:
Womanhood, manhood, chilehood, careerhood.
Dem is all jus a hat we put on we head,
And donn round like peacock in da tredd,
Till dat time is gone and we need to tekk anoda.

We duz grow out ta dem hoods.
We duz get too big fa dem hats.
Even dough dem duz feel comfortable.
Like a ol pair u shoes we duz like wearing.

Life duz change and we have ta too.
Dere's noting really we can do 'bout it, it's true.
But accept dat, dat is life.
And we can adjust ta it – easy and nice.
Not holeing on and struggling truu.

If you spen time holeling on,
You'll miss da good dat dere fah you - it gone!
You'll be missing out on all dee new,
And wonderful tings all bout round fah you.

So, realise and axcept dat life is a journey,
Don't fuget!
You here ta learn, ta love and ta be.
Always giving of all what de creator put widin ya see.

Life duz change, it duz change a lot.
So, enjoy everting you, while you got,
And when de next stage a your life begin,
Breath in and say tankya.
And jump right in.

A reflection on the many stages of life and the human desire for things to remain the same.

We crave stability and at the same time we need change.

We fight within ourselves, these two things that we cannot change.

Written in the Barbadian dialect.

Dis Skin I Living In

You see dis skin I living in?
Let me tell, it beautiful widout and widin.
De Creator Herself choose it fa me.
She knew dat wid in it, I'd be born free.

You see de beauty, dis colour it brings,
De power it promotes, de wisdom it sings?
Dis is a part of de journey chosen fah me,
To deliver her message of love, and strength and glee.
It's not every soul can carry such beauty,
It's not every spirit could live, so joyfully.

Each hue, each tone, each chosen spectrum,
It's gift with its own message will bring.
Some ting different and new of de Creator true.

You caan be me and I caan be you,
But when we love we self, we'll see what's true,
De Creator is made of multiplicity,
Of shades and colours, of 1, 2 and 3's.

You see dis skin I living in?
It's only a cover for the awesomeness wid in,
My job is ta love it, enjoy it and do all ta show,
Dat truu it, the glory of love and joy herself,
Transcends it, all.
Truu dis skin I living in.

*Written in the
Barbadian dialect
to celebrate
Black History Month
in the UK 2016.*

Satadee Cleaning

I spen de afternoon and mose a de day,
Cleaning, cleaning, cleaning dee dust and dee dirt away,
Wait, nu body else duz see de dirt?
Nu body else duz see de mess?
It's only me dat caan clean de best?
Is only me caan get nuh ress?

Who sa dat jus because I name woman,
Dat it's my job every Satadee morning
Tu scrub de house while ever body else jus chilling out?
I's de only one living in dis house?
I's de only one duz make de mess?

Dis Satadee morning cleaning duz seem ta have a voice.
Duz speak in a language, duz come ta live, bouy.

It stem back from de days when we did slaves,
And ha to clear de maasta house on Satadees.
Cause Satadee night dem usesta mak nuff noise,
Widd de partying and drinking and dancing 'bout.
So, as a slave ya din had na choice.

But now ya nowa, dis is my house,
And I doun hah to hear de massta voice.
I now hah me ownist choice.
To clean or not, dis is my house.
So, come Satadee morning,
I caan stay in me bed,
Ress me bones and relax instead.

I will clean me house, when I good and ready.
An if you doun like it, you got a choice.
You don't hafa come.
You caan stay where you is.
Or, you caan chose to clean my house instead.
I ain' gonn complain, I be happy.
You caan call me massta
I'll call you nanny.

Like many families from the Caribbean, Saturdays was the day for shopping and cleaning the house from top to bottom. And as you grew older it was your responsibility to the cleaning while your mother went out to do the shopping.
As I grew, like others, I continued the tradition for many years. Until one day I realised that I did have a choice as to when or whether or not I cleaned my house. Independence found its voice.

Written in the Barbadian dialect to pay homage to my heritage, customs and people.

To Go Forward

Going back is so part of going forward.
It's not possible to move forward,
Without knowing what's behind you.

At times, we see the past as gone,
But to create the future,
we need to know
That place of truth within who we are.
That place within ourselves, must be known

I'd forgotten so much of who I am,
Of what I was to be.
Looking back, has me back to where it is
I should be.

Reconnecting with who I am,
Is the answer I now seek.
Lost in the changes that life brings to meet.

Sometimes you cannot find yourself,
Through the lies of history's passing.

Going back is a part of my going forward,
Remembering who I am, who I was.
Finding me again through ancestry,
Through family, through true history,
Only then forward I will be.

Touch

Something is missing, even here,
Where love is protected and treasures shared.
Maybe my expectations, are indeed unreal,
What I'm wanting too severe.

I think I'm still growing up,
Still learning just how and what and where,
Is me and now.

I'm growing in this love affair,
Growing in all I've got to care,
How to balance things out, what's realistic,
What love's all about,
What it's not.

I know I'm so fortunate,
I know I have so much,
Everything I want is all right here
Within a reach, a touch.

What If

What if you could, holding nothing back?
Have whatever you wanted
At the drop of a hat?

Would you appreciate it?
Would you hold back?
Resist the temptation to trample the fat?

Would you hesitate or maybe think twice?
About your choices and other people's lives?

It's easy to wonder, it's easy to guess.
It's all maybe, make believe, at its very best.

Because we really never know,
Until we are there, in the very moment,
In the spot light, in the chair.

Looking towards it,
We'd probably destroy it, our world,
And our lives far sooner by it.
Without limitations to hold us back from doom.

What if it's not 20/20 vision,
It is only a dream, it's only a vision,
Of another life we could have built in between.

A life that maybe does exist in another dimension or field.
On another hill of where we could exist,
Somewhere, somehow, some place a far from this.

Where our what ifs do exist.
And we are in the ecstatics of happiness and bliss.

With You I am Alive

You make me feel alive,
You make me feel sexy,
Sexual and appealing,
You make me feel young,
Like a teenager again.

With you I'm the young girl,
That has always been
The one that changes, life,
And growing up hides.

You bring her to light,
You bring her to love,
You make her bold,
Confident, afflux.

You take me back to exploring who I am,
Exploring who I can still be,
You take me back to me.

You make me feel alive,
You wake me up again from the night
Physically, sexually, mentally, all that.
In love no pain. Just alive.

A Message To Somebody...

If you ask for opportunities,
Please note that the Universe will respond.
And guess what?
You will receive the opportunities to do
Or achieve or become just what you asked for.
When these opportunities arrive,
Please don't spend all your time and energy complaining,

That someone else has not done this or that for you.
Or that it's too hard or that you're not being helped.
No help is remaining.

You still have to do the work yourself.
This is how you will learn, grow and develop yourself,
For the next stage, your next big achievement.

If someone else does it all for you,
You cannot then claim the glory, praise or get the benefits.
You will then never be ready for your next great thing.
You will have given it away.
Please then do not be upset that you do not
Make progress in your life, business or career.
Start from where you are.
Start from here.

The butterfly has to break out of its cocoon itself.
No one else can do this is for it.

Or it will not have the strength to fly and
Give the rest of the world such
Pleasure to see it as it flutters by.
It is the same with your life.
So, I love you, but stop griping.
Start being thankful. And get on with your life.
Work to change and grow you into the best you, you can be.

Oh, look! Here comes another opportunity for you.
Get on with learning how to... Fly!

Artwork/images created by
© 2016 Jerusha Barnett-Cameron
All Rights Reserved

We all, at least most of us are frequenters of Facebook and its bombardment of stories, quotes and opinion. I felt somewhat frustrated with the moans and complaints of many who use this social media medium and thought I'd respond.

About the Author

Sandra Pollock is mother, wife, sister, and a multi-Award Winning Director with over 25 years' experience in leadership, management, people development and organisational change.

Her passion is people development and she has spent most of her life working with men and women all over the world sharing her inspiring and unique approach to confidence building, mindset and behavioural change. Sandra has worked in most sectors at corporate level.

Through her consultancy Open Mind Training & Development Ltd., Sandra works with CEOs, MDs and other senior management teams of organisations to help them to develop more effective use of their people (human resources) and improve their leadership skills and mindset.

Her outstanding business acumen, track record of achievement, professionalism and reputation as a 'go to' person, has gained a number of awards for her work in business and the community.

She is a dynamic motivational public speaker, contributes to publications on management, coaching and career development issues and is a regular guest on BBC Radio Leicester in the UK, a Radio and TV Presenter and Singer in her space time, when she is not writing poetry.

Sandra lives with her family in the UK and travels worldwide with her work as a speaker, coaching and business consultant.

Social Media Links

You can stay in touch with Sandra Pollock and find out what she is working on via social media.

Websites/Blogs:
www.sandrapollock.com

Facebook
https://www.facebook.com/sandra.pollock2

Twitter
@OpenMindCoach
https://twitter.com/OpenMindCoach

LinkedIn
https://www.linkedin.com/in/sandrapollock/

Pinterest
https://uk.pinterest.com/brainchildclear

Instagram
https://www.instagram.com/sandrampollock

SanRoo Publishing

SanRoo Publishing was set up by a mother and daughter team of writers, with the sole aim of encouraging budding writers, and to create a space where there is the freedom to create and publish their literature in the style, frequency they wanted, without breaking the bank or diminishing their creativity.

Sandra Pollock has written all her life but did not herself initially have the confidence to publish. When the lack of confidence was overcome, she then faced the mammoth task dealing with the closed door approach of the publishing industry. Her final frustrating realisation was that within the publishing environment very few female authors seemed able to break through into it.

After going the process of getting her daughter's first two books Vircover Petal (2010) and Rage (2012) published, followed by her own first book Making Changes That Grow Roots in 2012, the frustrations experienced by new and amateur writers were clearly understood. The pair vowed to create and publish their own works in the future. From their experiences, SanRoo Publishing was formed.

SanRoo is a small publishing space which aims to encourage writers of all genre and more importantly, all ages and genders, who wish to publish their work without the stress and frustration of larger publishers.

"Many of us may never achieve a best seller, but more of us, particularly women, have the creativity and tenancy to create something worth reading by 'the everyday' person. We should all be allowed the option to reach for our dreams no matter how small, large or how distant they may appear to us today." Sandra Pollock.

SanRoo is particularly interested in supporting female writers as the female written voice appears to be less published when you look at the percentages of published works across the whole of the arts, culture, film, and music industries. Our vision is to create a larger, more encouraging environment in the publishing arena for works by women and although we are open to working from all genders.

If you would like to find out more our SanRoo Publishing and how we might able to work with you we can be contacted via www.sanroopublishing.co.uk

www.ingramcontent.com/pod-product-compliance
Lightning Source LLC
Chambersburg PA
CBHW040336300426
44113CB00021B/2764